RITA BURNS SEN

When Your Child Becomes Catholic

What Parents and Sponsors Need to Know

ST. ANTHONY MESSENGER PRESS

Cincinnati, Ohio

Also by Rita Burns Senseman:

A Child's Journey:
The Christian Initiation of Children

Nihil Obstat: Rev. Thomas Richstatter, O.F.M., S.T.D.
         Rev. Robert L. Hagedorn

Imprimi Potest: Rev. Fred Link, O.F.M.
         Minister Provincial

Imprimatur: +Most Rev. Carl K. Moeddel
         Vicar General and Auxiliary Bishop
         Archdiocese of Cincinnati
         April 20, 2000

The *nihil obstat* and *imprimatur* are a declaration that a book or pamphlet is considered to be free from doctrinal or moral error. It is not implied that those who have granted the *nihil obstat* and *imprimatur* agree with the contents, opinions or statements expressed.

Cover illustration and book design by Constance Wolfer

ISBN 0-86716-375-5

Copyright © 2000, Rita Burns Senseman
All rights reserved.

Published by St. Anthony Messenger Press.
www.AmericanCatholic.org

Printed in the U.S.A.

Contents

Welcome!

The Catholic Christian community welcomes you! We are pleased to know that you are interested in this community for your child. We understand that you may have questions about how your child becomes a member of the Catholic Church and prepares for Baptism.

When Your Child Becomes Catholic will answer some of the most often-asked questions parents have about their school-age children being baptized and becoming Catholic. We hope you will find this information helpful. This brief booklet contains four parts:

- **PART ONE,** "Preparing for Baptism and Initiation Into the Catholic Church," answers the questions that parents most often ask regarding their children being baptized and initiated into the Catholic Church. It also describes the process of initiation and the parent's and child's involvement.

- **PART TWO,** "The Seven Sacraments of the Catholic Church," discusses the seven sacraments: the three sacraments of initiation, the two sacraments of healing and the two sacraments of commitment and vocation.

- **PART THREE,** "You and Your Child on the Journey of Faith," contains information and ideas for starting your child on the journey of Christian initiation, including how to integrate Catholic practices and prayers into your daily life.

- **PART FOUR,** "The Role of Sponsors and Sponsoring Families," identifies the roles and responsibilities of parish sponsors and sponsoring families. Each person interested in becoming Catholic is paired with a parish sponsor or sponsoring family. Part Four also provides information about the selection of godparents and sponsors.

We hope *When Your Child Becomes Catholic* will help you learn more about the Catholic Church and make you feel more at home with us. A member of our pastoral staff would be happy to talk with you about any questions or concerns not addressed in this booklet. Be assured that we will stay in close contact with you.

God's peace and blessing to you and your child as you begin the journey of faith!

PART ONE

Preparing for Baptism and Initiation Into the Catholic Church

I would like my child to be baptized. What should I do?

The Catholic Church welcomes you and your child and supports your desire for your child to become Catholic. Once you have decided to explore Baptism for your child, we ask you to meet with a staff person in the parish who will explain in more detail the process for preparing for Baptism and initiation into the Catholic Church.

We will ask you and your child to participate in the Catholic Church's process of welcoming new members called the Rite of Christian Initiation of Adults (often called the RCIA). The Rite of Christian Initiation of Adults is a process of initiation that prepares children and adults to receive the three sacraments of initiation: Baptism, Confirmation and Eucharist (or Communion). Part Two of this booklet, "The Seven Sacraments of the Catholic Church," on page 15, provides a closer look at the sacraments of initiation and four other sacraments.

My child is school-age. How old does a child have to be to participate in the RCIA?

Children who are approximately age seven or older prepare for Baptism by participating in the RCIA.

What will my child learn in the RCIA process?

The Church considers the Rite of Christian Initiation of Adults a journey on which your child will come to know more about God, Jesus, the Holy Spirit, the Bible, the sacraments and the teachings of the Catholic Church. We hope that your child will not only learn about God and the Church, but will deepen his or her relationship with God and feel at home in the Catholic Church.

What is involved in the RCIA journey?

To participate in the Rite of Christian Initiation of Adults, you and your child will be asked to attend some initiation sessions. During these initiation sessions you, your child and others interested in the Catholic Church will learn more about our faith and our Catholic Christian community. The initiation sessions will be a time for us to share with you our Catholic beliefs, traditions and stories. It also will be a time for you to ask questions and discuss issues important to you and your child. We ask that you, as the parent or guardian, walk the journey with your child, if possible.

I was born and raised as a Catholic. This process seems much different from the way things were done when I was young. When did this new way of preparing for Baptism begin?

During the Second Vatican Council (a worldwide meeting of Roman Catholic bishops held in the early 1960's), the Church reinstated the ancient tradition of Christian initiation called the *catechumenate*. This call for the reinstatement of the catechumenate led to the development of a universal document called the *Rite of Christian Initiation of Adults*.

As described earlier, the Rite of Christian Initiation of Adults is the way that adults and children over the age of seven prepare for the Sacraments of Baptism, Confirmation and Eucharist. Through these three sacraments of initiation, adults and children become full members of the Catholic Church. The bishops of the Second Vatican Council believed that the catechumenate was a more comprehensive way of preparing people for Baptism and initiation into the Church.

The Church still maintains the tradition of baptizing infants. Many children are baptized as infants in the Catholic Church, and they then celebrate First Communion and Confirmation when they are older. Whether baptized as an infant or as an older person, your child receives the fullness of God's grace. Both ways are perfectly acceptable, valid, good and holy in the eyes of the Church.

How long does the RCIA or initiation process take?

The amount of time it takes for a child to be initiated into the

Catholic Church differs for each child. The faith journey differs for each family. How long it takes depends upon your family history and how much religious formation your child has already had. It also depends upon how much familiarity your child and family have with the Catholic Christian community. Some families are new to the Catholic Church, and other families have been a part of the Catholic Church for years.

In the *Rite of Christian Initiation of Adults* the Church describes four periods, or phases, the child moves through on the way to Baptism and full initiation into the Church. Some children may pass through these four periods in a number of months; other children may take a number of years for their journey. There is no hurry! We want your child and you to take as much time as desired.

What are these four periods of the RCIA?

The first period, called the *Period of Evangelization and Precatechumenate*, is the time of **inquiry.** It is a time for you and your child to inquire or ask about the Catholic Church. During this time you and your child will hear many stories about the Catholic Church, our loving and generous God, our savior Jesus Christ and the Holy Spirit. You will hear stories from the Bible. You will be able to ask questions and to discuss whatever most interests you about our faith and our Church. We also hope that you and your child will share your story with us. Most importantly, this first period is a time for your child to develop a friendship with God and the Catholic Christian community.

After completing the first period of inquiry, your child will be invited to move to the second period of the initiation process, called the *Period of the Catechumenate.* This second period is a time for your child to **come to know more deeply the Catholic Christian way of life.** During the catechumenate your child (and you as well) will deepen his or her friendship with God, come to know Jesus Christ more fully, better understand God's Word—the Bible, become familiar with the basic teachings of the Catholic Church, and learn more about prayer and the community's life of service.

The third period of the initiation process, called the *Period of Purification and Enlightenment,* usually coincides with Lent. (Lent is the forty-day season just before Easter when Christians focus on prayer, fasting and almsgiving.) Children who enter the third period of the RCIA process are considered ready to celebrate the sacraments of initiation. The Period of Purification and Enlightenment is a time for children and adults to **complete their preparation for Baptism, Confirmation and Eucharist and for spiritual reflection in anticipation of initiation at Easter.**

The initiation of school-age children and adults usually happens at Easter. The children are baptized, confirmed and celebrate Eucharist at the Easter Vigil on Holy Saturday night (the night before Easter Sunday). Your child may be initiated this Easter or next Easter, or at another time, depending upon when your child is ready. The pastoral staff at our parish will help you decide what is best for your child and when he or she is ready for initiation.

After Easter comes the final period of Christian initiation, called the *Period of Mystagogy*. During this fourth period, you and your family will have time to sit back and think about everything that has happened on your journey of faith so far! It is a time to reflect upon the sacraments your child has received and look ahead to **living life as a baptized disciple of Jesus Christ.**

Can we baptize my child now and do the other sacraments later?

The sacraments of initiation—Baptism, Confirmation and Eucharist—are so closely united that the Church believes they should be celebrated together if the person to be initiated is age seven or older. Because your child is old enough to develop a personal faith in God and understand what he or she is doing, the Church believes that your child is old enough to be *fully* initiated into the Catholic Church. Fully initiated means your child will receive all three sacraments of initiation in keeping with the Church's ancient tradition of celebrating the Sacraments of Baptism, Confirmation and Eucharist at the same time. Although many children are baptized as infants with Confirmation and Eucharist delayed, your child has reached the age of reason and is therefore to be fully initiated at Easter.

What does a parent have to do during this process? What if a parent cannot be involved?

We ask that parents fully participate in the process of initiation if that is possible. This means we will ask you to attend some initiation sessions and to participate in some rites or ceremonies with your child. Although parental permission is the only thing that is required of parents in order for your child to be initiated into the Catholic Church, we hope that you will walk with your child on this journey of faith. We believe you will find the process of initiation rewarding and enriching for you as well as for your child. Often, families find that the process of initiation is an opportunity for the entire family to grow in faith.

The Church believes that parents are the primary persons who pass along faith to their children. If a parent cannot be actively involved in the initiation process, another family member, such as a grandparent, aunt or uncle, may bring the child to our initiation sessions. The parish may also pair your child with a sponsoring family if a parent or other adult family member cannot be present. Even if you can be present with your child, we may pair you with a sponsoring family to walk the journey with you. The most important concern is that the child have a supportive, loving adult to accompany him or her on the journey toward full initiation into the Catholic Church.

What are the rites or ceremonies of initiation?

Along the way to becoming Catholic, your child will be invited to celebrate certain rituals that mark progress toward Baptism, Confirmation and Eucharist. Each rite is a step toward full initiation into the Catholic Church. There are three major steps that your child may celebrate:

1. The first step (or rite) is called the *Rite of Acceptance into the Order of Catechumens*. This ritual is celebrated when your child completes a period of initial inquiry (Period of Evangelization and Precatechumenate). If your child has a desire to know more about God and the Church, then he or she is accepted as a *catechumen*—one who is preparing for Baptism.

2. The second step is called the *Rite of Election*. This ritual is celebrated when your child completes the second period of formation (Period of the Catechumenate). Your child is now "elected" by God to begin the final, more intense period of preparation for the sacraments of initiation.

3. The third step is the actual celebration of the sacraments of initiation: Baptism, Confirmation and Eucharist. This celebration usually occurs at Easter. After the celebration of the sacraments of initiation, there is one final period of post-Baptism formation— the Period of Mystagogy.

4. There are also minor rituals that your child may celebrate throughout the journey of initiation. These minor rites are celebrated during the second and third periods of formation.

We ask parents to be present for the rites so that they can present their children to the community and act as witnesses to the community about their children's intention. If a parent cannot be present, a sponsor will stand in to represent the parent.

When a child becomes Catholic, does one parent or both have to become Catholic, too?

No. Even though we ask parents to participate in the process of initiation and support your child as he or she grows and develops in faith, parents do not have to become Catholic themselves. If you feel you cannot support your child in this faith decision, we will ask a parish sponsor to act as your child's support person.

If a parent is interested in becoming a Catholic Christian, we will help connect you to our parish's Rite of Christian Initiation of Adults, the process for adults who wish to prepare for Baptism and initiation into the Church. We may ask you to attend some additional sessions for adults going through the RCIA.

My child is already baptized in another Christian denomination. What does my child need to do to become Catholic?

We ask that your child participate in the Rite of Christian Initiation of Adults. The RCIA is designed for adults and children who are preparing for Baptism, but it is also for baptized Christians who are seeking membership in the Catholic Church. We recognize that your child is already baptized, and we greatly respect the dignity of his or her Baptism. Your child will not be rebaptized as long as he or she was baptized with water and baptized in the name of the Trinity (in the name of God the Father, Son and Holy Spirit).

Much of what has already been said about children preparing for Baptism may apply to your previously bap-

tized child as well. Your child will be asked to attend some
sessions to learn more about the Catholic Church, and you
also will be asked to participate. Your child may also celebrate some of the rites (or ceremonies) that mark progress
on the journey to full initiation.

When the time comes for your child to be initiated into
the Catholic Church, he or she will make a profession of
faith and receive the Sacraments of Confirmation and
Eucharist. Children are often initiated into the Church
during the Easter season. Sometimes they are initiated at
the Easter Vigil on Holy Saturday night or on a Sunday of
the Easter Season. Depending upon the readiness of your
child, he or she may be initiated at a time other than the
Easter season.

My child was baptized Catholic as an infant, but we have not been to Church much since then. What do I need to do for my child to receive the other sacraments?

Your child may need to participate in the Rite of Christian
Initiation of Adults as described earlier. Even though your
child is already a member of the Catholic Church by virtue
of his or her baptism, your child has not put his or her
faith into practice. Thus, your child may have needs and
questions similar to other children who are new to the
Catholic Church. Depending on the age of your child and
the circumstances of your family, participating in the RCIA
may be the best way for your child to prepare for the celebration of Confirmation and Eucharist. However, since
your child is already baptized Catholic, other ways of

preparing for the sacraments might be considered. Our pastoral staff will be happy to talk with you about what is best for your child.

My child has friends in the religious education classes at this parish. Can my child join these Catholic friends in class?

We respect the desires and individuality of each child. While some children and adolescents are very comfortable in classes with their baptized Catholic peers, others feel more comfortable waiting until they have had more experience in the Catholic Church. We ask that you and your child think about attending our religious education classes. Please know that these religious education classes are designed primarily for baptized Catholic children. Depending upon the age of your child and your child's experience with the Church, the classes may or may not be a good fit at this point.

We ask that your child participate in the RCIA sessions. We will talk with you more about our religious education program and help you decide if those classes would also be helpful for your child.

Can my child celebrate First Communion (or Confirmation) with her friends?

When your child becomes a Catholic Christian, she will celebrate the Sacraments of Baptism, Confirmation and Eucharist. The Church strongly believes in the unity of the three sacraments of initiation. When a child has reached the age of reason (approximately age seven), the Church believes the child is old enough to receive and nurture a personal faith and, thus, is to be fully initiated by receiving all three sacraments of initiation.

If your child would also like to participate in the parish celebration of First Communion or Confirmation with her parish friends, that can usually be arranged. Often, parish celebrations of First Communion and Confirmation occur during the Easter season, which would fall after your child has already received her First Communion and Confirmation. Although your child could still receive the Eucharist at a First Communion celebration, she would not be confirmed again with her friends. Confirmation is a sacrament that is not repeated.

What happens after my child has received the sacraments and become Catholic?

After your child has received the sacraments of initiation and become a member of the Catholic Church, he or she will participate in the parish religious education program along with the other children and adolescents of the parish. After your child has been initiated, we ask that you register your child in our religious education classes. By this time your child will know many of his or her peers in the parish and we hope will feel at home. Your child will continue growing in faith and learning about the Catholic Church all through life. Our belief is that the celebration of the sacraments of initiation is one important milestone in a lifelong journey of conversion to Jesus Christ. We hope that your child will participate in faith formation opportunities and religious education activities throughout your years here at our parish and beyond.

It is very important for the spiritual development of your child to continue his or her religious formation, even though your child will have received the three sacraments of initiation. At times, your child's friends may be preparing for sacraments that your child has already received. Your child will still participate in our religious education programs even after receiving the sacraments. Perhaps your child will help friends who are preparing for Confirmation and Eucharist!

Do we need to go to church every Sunday since we are not yet Catholic?

We believe that coming to church to worship with us is one of the best ways for your child to get to know our loving God and our Catholic Christian community. Celebrating with our community on Sunday will introduce your child to the Catholic way of life. You will have the opportunity to pray with us and to listen to God's Word proclaimed. Also, coming to Mass—our Sunday worship service— will help you get to know other members of our parish.

As your child begins the second part of the initiation process (the Period of the Catechumenate), he or she will be asked to come to Mass each week to hear the Word of God proclaimed. After listening to the readings from the Bible and the priest's homily (a homily is like a sermon), children preparing for sacramental initiation are dismissed from the main church to meet in another place to talk about the Word of God. We call this time "Breaking Open the Word" because it is a time when children learn about God's Word and how to apply it to their lives.

Coming to church each week to hear the Word of God helps your child prepare for the day when he or she will come to the altar to receive the Body and Blood of Christ in the Eucharist (also called Communion). For fully initiated members of the Catholic Church, coming to church each Sunday to celebrate the Eucharist is central to who we are and all we do.

What happens if I cannot bring my child to church on Sunday or to the sessions?

If you are unable to bring your child to church each week, our parishioners can help. A sponsor or a sponsoring family from our parish will be paired with your child and you during the journey of initiation. Your sponsor or sponsoring family will be able to help you and your child get to church and to the RCIA sessions.

PART TWO

The Seven Sacraments of the Catholic Church

What is a sacrament?

A sacrament is a visible sign of God's presence. We believe that through the signs and symbols of the sacraments—water, oil, bread and wine, laying on of hands—God communicates with us. Then, we in turn respond to God's communication. The seven sacraments are sacred celebrations of the Church in which we encounter God.

You may have heard some Catholics say that "sacraments give grace." This means that sacraments communicate to us God's presence. "Grace" is a word used to describe God's presence in our lives.

What are the seven sacraments of the Catholic Church?

There are three sacraments of initiation—Baptism, Confirmation and Eucharist; two sacraments of healing—

Reconciliation (or Penance) and Anointing of the Sick; and two sacraments of commitment and vocation— Marriage and Holy Orders.

What are the sacraments of initiation?

Baptism, Confirmation and Eucharist are the three sacraments of initiation. These three sacraments combine to bring us fully into union with Jesus Christ and give us full membership in the Catholic Church. When a person is age seven or older, he or she receives all three sacraments of initiation at the same time. When a person is age seven or older and is preparing to receive the sacraments of initiation, the person is initiated according to the *Rite of Christian Initiation of Adults*. When persons are younger than age seven, they are baptized according to the *Rite of Baptism for Children*. They then celebrate Confirmation and Eucharist when they are older.

What is the Sacrament of Baptism?

Baptism unites us to Christ. Baptism is the first sacrament of initiation. Through the waters of Baptism we are united with Jesus Christ. Those united with Christ in Baptism share fully in the mystery of his death and resurrection. In Baptism we live eternally with Jesus Christ.

Baptism gives us new life. By plunging into the living waters of Baptism, a person is born anew. In Baptism we become a new creation through the power of the Holy

Spirit. We become children of God. The waters of life give us a new beginning as God's daughters and sons. As newly created children of God, we also are members of the Church—God's family, God's people. Thus, through Baptism, not only do we have new life in Christ, we have a new life in the Church.

Baptism cleanses us. The waters of Baptism cleanse us and give us a new beginning. All sin is washed away, and we begin life anew as children of God. As we go down into the holy waters of Baptism, we bury our sins with Christ so we can rise with him in glory. After being washed clean, we are clothed in glory and given the light of Christ to burn forever in our hearts.

What is the Sacrament of Confirmation?

Confirmation fills us with the Holy Spirit. Confirmation is the second sacrament of initiation. In the Sacrament of Confirmation we are signed with a sacred oil called *chrism*, and the Holy Spirit is poured out fully upon us. The Holy Spirit strengthens us to live as children of God united to Jesus Christ through Baptism. We receive the full outpouring of the gifts of the Holy Spirit: the spirit of wisdom and understanding, the spirit of right judgment and courage, the spirit of knowledge and reverence, and the spirit of wonder and awe.

Confirmation makes us more like Jesus Christ. In Confirmation we are anointed and made to be more like Christ. By filling us with the Holy Spirit we are made more

completely in the image of Christ Jesus so that we can do
God's work here on earth. After Baptism we are sealed with
the sacred oil to help us live faithfully and actively as members of the Church, members of the Body of Christ.

What is the Sacrament of Eucharist?

**In Eucharist we receive the Body and
Blood of Jesus Christ.** Eucharist is the third sacrament of
initiation, the culminating point of one's initiation into the
Church. Having been washed clean in Baptism and sealed
with the Holy Spirit in Confirmation, we now come to the
table of the Eucharist. At the table, we eat the body and
drink the blood of Jesus Christ. The Body and Blood of
Jesus Christ is the gift of our salvation. The Eucharist is
the climax of our union with Jesus Christ and the Church.

In the Eucharist we share in Jesus Christ's sacrifice.
By sacrificing himself on the cross, Jesus won for us the
forgiveness of our sins and life everlasting. In the Eucharist,
we remember his sacrifice and the salvation he won for us.
As we recall his sacrifice, he is once again present with us.
Through the prayers of the priest and the power of the
Holy Spirit, the bread and wine become the Body and
Blood of Christ Jesus, our Lord.

In the Eucharist we share a meal. The Eucharist is
a meal which shows forth our unity with God and God's
people, the Church. We come together as one family, united in Christ, and we eat and drink the Body and Blood of
Christ. This holy meal is also a remembrance of Jesus' last

meal with the disciples. At the table we remember that Jesus gave us his body and blood at the Last Supper and told the disciples to continue his work on earth by serving and helping others. The Eucharist nourishes us with Christ's own body so that we have the strength we need to continue Jesus' work on earth.

The Eucharist, also known as Mass or Communion, is the worship service we celebrate on Sunday. Here we listen to selected readings from the Bible, and we receive the Body and Blood of Christ. Catholics sometimes say *Eucharist* when referring only to the bread and wine, or body and blood. The partaking of the Body and Blood of Christ is also called *Communion*. In many parishes, Eucharist or Mass, is celebrated during the week as well as on Sunday.

What is the Sacrament of Reconciliation?

In the Sacrament of Reconciliation (also called Penance or Confession), the Church celebrates healing through the forgiveness of sin. Sin breaks one's relationship with God, with the community and with self. In the Sacrament of Reconciliation, the Church celebrates the forgiveness of sin and the mending of one's relationship with God, community and self.

In the Sacrament of Reconciliation, a person confesses his or her sins to a priest. The priest gives a human voice to God's loving mercy. As a representative of Jesus Christ and the Christian community, the priest forgives the person in the name of God.

What is the Sacrament of the Anointing of the Sick?

In the Sacrament of the Anointing of the Sick, the Church prays that God will give the sick person help, strength and peace. The person who is sick is anointed on the forehead and hands with the sacred oil of the sick. In this sacrament of healing, the community recalls Jesus' suffering and prays that the one who is sick will receive hope, courage and healing. Like all the sacraments, Anointing of the Sick is meant to be a community celebration.

What is the Sacrament of Marriage?

The Sacrament of Marriage, a sacrament of vocation, celebrates the sacred union of wife and husband. In the Sacrament of Marriage a woman and man enter a covenant or promise. In this covenant they commit themselves to each other for life, a promise unbreakable in the eyes of the Church. In married life the woman and man love each other totally and completely and help each other to be holy people.

What is the Sacrament of Holy Orders?

The other sacrament of vocation, the Sacrament of Holy Orders, is one by which a man is ordained a priest in order to serve all the baptized. The priest is a minister and leader in the Church. Through Holy Orders a priest is sealed with the Holy Spirit and acts in the name and person of Jesus Christ. The priest is a minister of the seven sacraments.

PART THREE

You and Your Child on the Journey of Faith

What kinds of things should I do at home to help my child on this journey of faith?

We offer some practical ideas for the ongoing religious formation and spiritual development of your child in your home. Please adapt them to your own needs and family situation.

1. **Read Bible stories with your child.** Most children like to be read to, even some older children! Teens, however, may prefer to read the stories themselves. Set aside a time each day or several times a week that is convenient for everyone and read the Bible together. Choose a place in the home that is quiet and comfortable. If you do not have a Bible, let us know. A parish staff person would be glad to give you a Bible and show you how to use it. If you have a young child, you may want to get a children's Bible.

We recommend starting your reading with these stories from the Bible—Old Testament and New Testament. You should feel free to explore other stories, of course! A parish staff person would be happy to recommend other stories, too.

After reading a story with your child, you should try to talk about it together. These questions might be helpful in starting discussion:

- What did you like best about the story? Why?
- What character did you like the best? Why?
- What message do you think God was trying to give in this story?
- What do you think God might be saying to you in this story?

OLD TESTAMENT STORIES

The story of creation ....*Genesis 1:1-2:3*
God calls Abraham and Sarah;
    the beginnings of the Israelites ....*Genesis 12:1-9*
The story of the Exodus; God saving
   the Hebrew people from slavery
   in Egypt...*Exodus 1-14*
The crossing of the Red Sea.................*Exodus 14:1-15:21*
The Ten Commandments...........................*Exodus 19-20*
The Israelites enter the Promised Land ......*Joshua 1:1-10*
The story of Ruth, great-grandmother
    of King David...*Ruth 1-4*
King David, ancestor of
    Jesus ....*2 Samuel 5:1-5, 2 Samuel 7:18-29*

A Song of David ....*Psalm 23*
A Song of Praise ....*Psalm 118*
Words from the Prophet Isaiah ....*Isaiah 49:1-6*
Words from the Prophet Jeremiah ....*Jeremiah 1:4-10*

NEW TESTAMENT STORIES
The birth of Jesus...*Luke 2:1-20*
Mary and her cousin Elizabeth.....................*Luke 1:5-80*
The wise men visit Jesus ....*Matthew 2*
Jesus lost in the temple ....*Luke 2:41-52*
John the Baptist baptizes Jesus ....*Matthew 3*
Jesus calls disciples ....*Luke 5:1-11*
Jesus at a wedding...*John 2:1-12*
Jesus heals a man who cannot walk ....*Mark 2:1-12*
Jesus teaches on a mountain...................*Matthew 5:1-16*
Jesus heals a person who cannot talk ....*Mark 7:31-35*
Jesus the good shepherd..........*John 10:1-16, Luke 15:4-6*
The Last Supper ....*Matthew 26:1-29*
Jesus dies on the cross............................*John 18 and 19*
Jesus' Resurrection...*John 20*
Breakfast on the beach ....*John 21:1-19*

2. **Pray with your child.** Children most often learn to pray by praying with a parent. You can begin by simply reading to your child some of the Catholic prayers included here. Eventually, your child will begin to take them to heart, and you will no longer need a book. At first, don't worry about trying to explain what all the words mean. Your child will let you know when he or she wants to talk about the meaning of the words. For

now, choose one or two prayers here and begin to say them together at bedtime or mealtime or whenever seems like the right time. If you have an older child, you might start by introducing a prayer before mealtime (even if family meals are few and far between!). Or, write some prayers on index cards or photocopy these and give them to your teenager. Leave them at his or her bedside and let your child decide when to pray.

You also may suggest that your older child start a journal. Give your child a notebook with the invitation to write down anything he or she would like to say to God. Your child may want to thank God or ask God for help or just write down random thoughts to God. Reassure your child that you will not read the journal unless you ask permission first.

CATHOLIC PRAYERS

The Lord's Prayer (or Our Father)

Our Father, who art in heaven,
hallowed be thy name;
thy kingdom come,
thy will be done on earth as it is in heaven.
Give us this day our daily bread;
and forgive us our trespasses
as we forgive those who trespass against us;
and lead us not into temptation,
but deliver us from evil.
Amen.

Hail Mary

Hail Mary, full of grace!
The Lord is with you;
blessed are you among women,
and blessed is the fruit of your womb, Jesus.
Holy Mary, Mother of God,
pray for us sinners,
now and at the hour of our death. Amen.

Glory to the Father (The Lesser Doxology)

Glory be to the Father,
and to the Son,
and to the Holy Spirit:
as it was in the beginning,
is now, and ever shall be,
world without end.
Amen.

Sign of the Cross

Catholics often begin and end prayers by making the Sign of the Cross. Trace a cross on yourself while saying:

In the name of the Father *(touch your right fingers on forehead)*,

and of the Son *(touch your right hand on heart)*,

and of the Holy Spirit *(touch your right hand on left shoulder, then on right shoulder)*.

Amen *(fold hands together in front)*.

Apostles' Creed

I believe in God, the Father almighty,
    creator of heaven and earth.
I believe in Jesus Christ, his only Son, our Lord.
    He was conceived by the power of the Holy Spirit
        and born of the Virgin Mary.
    He suffered under Pontius Pilate,
        was crucified, died, and was buried.
    He descended to the dead.
        On the third day, he rose again.
    He ascended into heaven,
        and is seated at the right hand of the Father.
    He will come again to judge the living and the dead.
I believe in the Holy Spirit,
    the holy catholic Church,
    the communion of saints,
    the forgiveness of sins,
    the resurrection of the body,
    and the life everlasting.
    Amen.

The Nicene Creed

We believe in one God,
    the Father, the Almighty,
    maker of heaven and earth,
    of all that is seen and unseen.
We believe in one Lord, Jesus Christ,
    the only Son of God,

eternally begotten of the Father,
God from God, Light from Light,
true God from true God,
begotten, not made, one in Being with the Father.
Through him all things were made.
For us men and for our salvation
    he came down from heaven:
by the power of the Holy Spirit
    he was born of the Virgin Mary, and became man.
For our sake he was crucified under Pontius Pilate;
    he suffered, died, and was buried.
On the third day he rose again
    in fulfillment of the Scriptures;
he ascended into heaven
    and is seated at the right hand of the Father.
He will come again in glory
    to judge the living and the dead,
and his kingdom will have no end.
We believe in the Holy Spirit, the Lord, the giver of life,
    who proceeds from the Father and the Son.
    With the Father and the Son he is worshiped and
        glorified.
    He has spoken through the Prophets.
    We believe in one holy catholic and apostolic Church.
    We acknowledge one baptism for the forgiveness
        of sins.
    We look for the resurrection of the dead,
    and the life of the world to come.
    Amen.

Prayer Before Meals

Bless us, O Lord, and these your gifts,
which we are about to receive,
from your goodness.
Through Christ our Lord.
Amen.

Prayer After Meals

We give you thanks for all your gifts, almighty God,
living and reigning now and forever.
(And may the souls of the faithful departed,
through the mercy of God, rest in peace.)
Amen.

Prayer to the Guardian Angel

Angel of God, my guardian dear,
to whom God's love commits me here,
ever this day be at my side,
to light and guard, to rule and guide.
Amen.

Act of Contrition

My God, I am sorry for my sins with all my heart.
In choosing to do wrong and failing to do good,
I have sinned against you whom I should love
    above all things.
I firmly intend, with your help, to do penance, to sin
    no more, and to avoid whatever leads me to sin.
Our Savior Jesus Christ suffered and died for us.
    In his name, my God, have mercy.

Jesus Prayer

Lord Jesus Christ, Son of God,
have mercy on me, a sinner.

Confiteor ("I Confess," from the Mass)

I confess to almighty God,
    and to you, my brothers and sisters,
        that I have sinned through my own fault
        in my thoughts and in my words,
        in what I have done,
        and in what I have failed to do;
    and I ask the blessed Mary, every virgin,
        all the angels and saints,
    and you, my brothers and sisters,
        to pray for me to the Lord our God.

3. **Come to church with your child.** One of the best ways for your child to get to know the Catholic Christian community is to come to church on Sunday. Being with us on Sunday is a good way for you to find out who we are and what we believe. Our worship service, called the Mass, may seem different to your child at first, but we believe your child will enjoy it and benefit from participating. There are two main parts to the Mass:

   ▪ *The Liturgy of the Word.* The first part of Mass focuses on the Word of God. After an opening song and some opening prayers, we listen to readings from the Bible. We usually hear three readings and sing a psalm. The priest then gives a homily to explain the readings and help connect them to our own experience. Then, we pray for our intentions and recite our creed.

▪ *The Liturgy of the Eucharist.* The second part of Mass centers around the offering of bread and wine which become the Body and Blood of Jesus Christ. Members of the community come forward to receive the Body and Blood of Christ. We end with a closing prayer and song. Then, the priest-celebrant sends us forth to do the work of Jesus Christ in the world.

After Mass you will have the opportunity to meet and talk with members of our parish. You are welcome and encouraged to come to church at other times, too. During the week our parish has time for prayer and social and community service activities. Your sponsor or sponsoring family can help you find out which activities might interest you and your child.

Part Four

The Role of Sponsors and Sponsoring Families

What is a sponsor or a sponsoring family?

A sponsor or a sponsoring family is an individual or a
family selected from our parish to be the companion to a
child participating in the RCIA. The sponsor or sponsoring
family is the "parish friend" for a child age seven or older
who is seeking Baptism, Confirmation and Eucharist.
The initiation family (the child seeking initiation and the
child's parent) may be paired with an individual sponsor
or a sponsoring family. From here on, we will use the phrase
sponsoring family to refer to an individual or a family with
more than one person.

In the *Rite of Christian Initiation of Adults* the Church asks
that sponsors from the Christian community accompany
candidates who are seeking Baptism, Confirmation and
Eucharist. The sponsoring family walks with the initiation
family on the journey of initiation.

If one or both parents cannot participate with their child in the process of initiation, the sponsoring family may be asked to stand in for the parents—to come to the sessions with the child and stand up with the child at the liturgical rites.

What does a sponsoring family do?

Foremost, the sponsoring family is a *companion* for the child seeking initiation and the child's family. Being a companion means "walking the walk" with the child and the child's family. It means "being there" for the child who has asked for Baptism. As a companion, the sponsoring family comes to the initiation sessions that the child and the child's family will be asked to attend. In addition, being a companion means being available to talk about concerns and questions the family may have, to listen when the child or parent has doubts, uncertainties, joys or jubilations regarding their new and developing faith life.

Second, a sponsoring family is a kind of *minister of hospitality.* Sponsoring families help the initiation family feel welcome in the parish and with the Catholic way of life. People are chosen to be sponsors because they possess a good sense of hospitality and welcome. The sponsoring family introduces the initiation family to Catholic traditions and customs. The sponsoring family extends gracious hospitality in the same way that Jesus would.

Third, the sponsoring family is asked to serve as a *witness* for the child seeking initiation. As friends who have "walked the walk" with the child and the child's family, the sponsoring family can witness to the child's desire for initiation. During a liturgical ritual called the Rite of Acceptance into the Order of Catechumens, the sponsoring family witnesses to the parish community that the child is sincere in intention and is ready to proceed in preparing for Baptism. The sponsoring family also may stand up with the candidate at a later time.

Fourth, the sponsoring family is a *model* of faith for the initiation family. They are a living example every day of how a Christian family follows the way of Jesus Christ in the Catholic tradition. By sharing faith, by sharing stories, by being in one another's company, by praying and worshipping together, the sponsoring family will model for the child and the initiation family how a Catholic Christian family lives and operates. By being in the company of active and committed Catholic Christians, you and your child will learn the Christian way of life.

What are the specific responsibilities of a sponsoring family?

A sponsoring family is asked to:

- Make an initial contact with the inquiring family by telephone or in person.
- Welcome the child and parent(s) with warmth and openness.
- Attend the initiation sessions with the initiation family.
- Spend some informal time getting to know the initiation family.

- Invite them to coffee and doughnuts after Mass.
- Invite them to a parish social event, service activity or community prayer service.
- Plan a family outing in the community or meet for dinner.
- Share faith by sharing stories.
- Share family prayer traditions and other Catholic customs.
- Introduce the initiation family to other people in the parish.
- Introduce the initiation family to parish traditions and events.
- Be a good example of a practicing Catholic family.
- Be a model of a praying, worshipping Catholic family.
- Be a guide in the Christian way of life and service by providing good example.
- Listen to the needs and concerns of the initiation family.
- Offer support along the way.
- Present the child candidate at the various liturgical rites.
- Give witness to the child's readiness at the rites.
- Be genuine. Be sincere. Be a friend!

What does the sponsoring family do at the rites?

At the first major rite in the process of initiation, the sponsoring family stands with the parent as they present the child to the parish community for the first time. The parish community welcomes those candidates who are preparing for sacramental initiation. Although it is the parent who presents the child for acceptance by the community, the sponsoring family's presence at the rite says to the parish, "We know this child, and we can testify to the child's faith and good intention."

If members of the sponsoring family are asked to be godparents, they would also stand up with the candidate at the Rite of Election and at the celebration of the sacraments.

Is a sponsor or sponsoring family the same thing as godparents?

A parish sponsor or sponsoring family is NOT the same thing as a godparent. A child preparing for Baptism needs to have godparents. A godparent is someone chosen by the family and child. The family may wish to choose a godmother, a godfather or both. At least one of the godparents must be a practicing Catholic, at least sixteen years of age, who has received all three sacraments of initiation: Baptism, Confirmation and Eucharist. The godparents must be in good standing with the Catholic Church and free to carry out the office of godparent.

Furthermore, godparents help the parents as the child grows and develops in faith. Godparents assist in the final phase of preparation for Baptism, and they continue in their role throughout the child's lifetime. The godparents, along with the parents, present the child at the Rite of Election, the doorway to the final period of preparation for Baptism. The godparents testify as to the child's readiness for Baptism.

When the time comes to celebrate Baptism, an initiation family may decide to choose the parish sponsor as a godparent, or they may choose someone else. Whoever is chosen to be the child's godparents, the parish sponsoring family will continue to support the initiation family as long as the child is preparing for the sacraments of initiation. We hope, however, that the sponsoring family and the initiation family will form a friendship that will last well beyond the initiation process.

Glossary

As you and your child begin the journey toward full initiation in the Church, you will hear some language that may sound unfamiliar. Below you will find a list of common words used in Church circles. If you hear a word being used that is not listed here, please ask a staff person or parishioner what it means. We will be happy to talk with you about it.

Candidate: A person who is already baptized and is preparing to be received into the Church. A baptized candidate receives the Sacraments of Confirmation and Eucharist when he or she is received into the Church. Sometimes, the Church uses this name for anyone who is preparing for any of the sacraments.

Catechumen: A person who is preparing for Baptism, Confirmation and Eucharist; a person in the second period of the initiation process, the Period of the Catechumenate.

Catechumenate: The second period in the process of initiation, the period that follows the Rite of Acceptance into the Order of Catechumens. The Church says that this time is to last "at least" one year.

CCD: These letters stand for Confraternity of Christian Doctrine, and refer to the religious education program in a parish. This program is sometimes called RE for religious education, or REP for religious education program, or PSR for public school of religion.

Communion: The bread and wine that has become the Body and Blood of Jesus Christ. When we receive Communion, sometimes called Eucharist, we are receiving the body and blood of Christ.

DRE: These letters stand for director of religious education, a staff member of the parish who is the minister and administrator of all religious education in the parish.

Elect: A person preparing for Baptism and in the third period of the initiation process, the Period of Purification and Enlightenment. Those who have celebrated the Rite of Election are considered the elect.

Eucharist: The Body and Blood of Jesus Christ. Eucharist also refers to our worship service called Mass, where we receive bread and wine which has become the Body and Blood of Christ. See Communion above.

Initiation: The welcoming or receiving of new members into the Church. We welcome or "initiate" new members by celebrating the Sacraments of Baptism, Confirmation and Eucharist.

Inquirer: A person interested in learning about the Catholic faith; one who is in the first period of the initiation process, called the Period of Evangelization and Precatechumenate, or Period of Inquiry.

Lectionary: A book containing selected readings from the Bible that are read during Mass and other liturgical celebrations.

Liturgy: Public worship in the Catholic Church. This word is sometimes used to refer to Mass or Eucharist.

Mystagogy: The fourth period in the process of initiation, lasting the seven weeks of the Easter season and extending to the first anniversary of a person's initiation.

Precatechumenate: The first period in the process of initiation, lasting an indefinite amount of time. It is sometimes called the inquiry period.

Purification and Enlightenment: The third period in the process of initiation, usually corresponding to the season of Lent, a six-week period prior to Easter.

RCIA: These letters stand for the *Rite of Christian Initiation of Adults*, a Church document that describes the way in which new members are welcomed into the Catholic Church.

RE: These letters stand for religious education. See CCD.

Rite: A ritual celebration in the Church.

Sacrament: A visible sign of God's presence. There are seven sacraments in the Catholic Church: Baptism, Confirmation, Eucharist, Reconciliation, Anointing of the

Sick, Marriage and Holy Orders. They are ritual celebrations of the Catholic community.

Sacraments of initiation: Baptism, Confirmation and Eucharist are the three sacraments of initiation. Through the celebration of the three sacraments a person is fully initiated into the Catholic Church. The person who receives these three sacraments is a full member of the Catholic Church.

YM: These letters stand for youth minister or youth ministry in the parish.

NOTES

_____
_____
_____
_____
_____
_____
_____
_____
_____
_____
_____
_____
_____
_____
_____
_____
_____
_____
_____
_____
_____
_____
_____